Language Acquisit

Building a solid foundation and pursuing a new level of language mastery

Steve Gill
Ushani Nanayakkara

Introduction

This short booklet has two very distinct parts. The first part focuses on building the foundation needed for a language learner (you or your student) to have faster and more successful learning. This section of the booklet is broken into five sections: What, How, Why, Author, and Notes. The emphasis is on knowing what to do, how to do it, and why you would do it that way. The foundation of language learning is only the beginning, but like a house, is critical to the future. The foundation not only lays out a pathway toward success, but it can also provide the learner (student or adult) with the personally relatable reasons to learn the language and the joy of learning the new language. These two components are critical to success.

The second section of this booklet is about helping to lay out a future path, post foundation, that is likely to lead to ongoing learning and success. This is different for every learner; therefore, this section of the booklet is broken into small sections that provide different learners a variety of information that they can use, helping them find the path that is their path.

Many of the items or strategies noted within the booklet can fill an entire book on their own. Please, if you read something that you want to know more about, go for it. This booklet is purposefully short to hit upon key, core areas that are practical and implementable.

Please exchange the words "you" and "your student" as is needed for your reading. That is, if you are reading this as a teacher to help a student, read "you" as "your student." If you are reading this as a language learning, then read "your student" as "you."

Part One

Foundational Language Acquisition
Taking individual language learning strategies and applying those to systems level actions that are simple and applicable

The focus of this section is on teaching English learners in our schools, but the techniques come from individual language learning. Also, this is about building a powerful foundation for future high-level learning. In an effort to be practical, the actions come first, then the how, the why, and finally, who is this guy writing this booklet. To some extent, this is backwards with regards to popular approaches to writing.

The Actions

Each of these actions are in reference to what/how to acquire, or assist others in acquiring, the noted skill or area.

1) Have the students master the first 750* most frequently used words as fast as possible
2) Learn or expose the learner in a crawl, walk, run model
3) Learn or expose the learner to the letter sounds, focusing on differences and tricks for mastery
4) Utilize technology as a tool every day, but not as a substitute for a teacher
5) Have the students reading ASAP (kindergarten books until mastered, then first grade books until mastered... and so on)
6) Focus on present tense (until they have mastered the first 1500 words)
7) Have the students master the next 750 (751-1500) most frequently used words
8) Create a "cheat" sheet with the students
9) Don't correct grammar or pronunciation, unless absolutely necessary (follow the crawl, walk, run model)

*This is based upon computer analysis and not ivory tower wisdom.

This could sound like a lot of work, finding or creating information, but the result can be used by other students in the following classes. Also, I am using "learn" or "expose the learner to" instead of "teach" in a purposeful manner that is discussed in the second section.

The "Hows"

Now, let's dive into the "hows" of this. Not deep into the woods, but enough to get started. The "why" comes later.

1. Master the first 750 most frequently used words as fast as possible

To get this list of words, you can search the Internet (at least 2 searches and some comparisons) or you can buy a book on this topic. However, if you buy a book, you need to make sure that they created the list through computer analysis (for the curious minds, there is a note and a reference about this at the end of the section).

First, go through the Rosetta Stone lessons (I use Rosetta Stone as an example later in this booklet, but this applies to any technology you are using to augment vocabulary development), and find the words from 101-750 most frequently used words that are already within the program. In other words, have your list of the most frequently used 750 words at your side. As you work through your chosen program and find the words that the program presents to the students within the first few hours of lessons, cross them off of the list.

Then, if a word is a noun or verb and not in the program, find a picture that matches the noun or verb, and make these cards. Also, you can buy premade cards and there will be a significant overlap (greatly reducing your work).

Last, for the first one hundred words, you need to make cards and get the students to learn these words yesterday! These are often connecting words that create a great deal of confusion (the the's, and's, or's and but's of the language). I say "often" for folks who are looking at this to learn a language other than English or I would have just listed them. There are many sources that indicate that the first 100 words make up roughly 50% of all spoken and written language.

2. Learn or Expose the learner in a crawl, walk, run model

All learning comes in stages, and not following those stages leads to frustration and poor learning. So, being able to crawl is learning those first 750 words and using books where the pictures match the words exactly. Being able to walk is knowing those next 750 words (likely more, given the nature of learning and living within the environment for our language learners). Also, the ability to express past, present, and future with a few more words and better understanding, and being able to read books in which the pictures might not be a perfect match (and might not even be there as you move toward running). Last, running is about expanding that vocabulary so that your speech has more depth and you can read with understanding more subtle meaning. And, you are starting to write sentences with more than a noun, a verb and simple helper words.

Please remember that part one of this booklet is focused on the first stages of language learning. There are many methods and approaches once the learner is at the "run" stage, and these tend to work best if personal preferences are taken into account. I am an avid reader; therefore, reading has been my pathway to higher level of Spanish and maintenance of my skills. Some experts put a heavy emphasis on academic conversations. I believe that the emphasis should remain on vocabulary and reading at first, then can shift to either focusing on reading or academic conversations (or other methods) once the foundation is strong enough.

3. Learn or Expose the Learner to the letter sounds, focusing on differences and tricks for mastery

It is likely that the majority of the letters will make the same sound (or a very similar sound) as in English. Then, focus on the letters that make the different sounds. For example, teaching a person coming from Spanish to English things like the following: H makes a sound, LL doesn't make a Y sound (it makes an L sound), E does not always sound like long A. In contrast, teaching a person coming from English to Spanish things like the following: H makes no sound, LL sounds like Y, E sounds like long A.

To achieve this, you might need an interpreter the first time you do it for a new language, then make sure to keep the list of letters/sounds for later students. Work with the interpreter to go through each of the letters, common blends, and diphthongs and triphthongs. You might miss some the first time, but getting the majority of these is the beginning to a great "cheat" sheet.

4. Utilize technology as a tool every day, not as a teacher

There are many potential programs and there are even more opinions regarding which one is the best. For the purposes of this discussion, I will talk about Rosetta Stone. Rosetta Stone does an amazing job of offering the student a way to see the words across multiple pictures and therefore letting the brain absorb the words. This is a tool, not a teacher. The students need to have a minimum exposure to this that corresponds to their age. In other words, there are not too many kindergarten age students who could use these types of programs successfully (Imagine Learning might be more kindergarten friendly, it was the last time I saw it). If a kindergarten student can use it, they might need supervision/instruction and should have their time limited to about 10-minute sessions, multiple sessions per day. Then, this can continue on up to high school students in increments of growth. For example, as a highly motivated adult my limit is about 1 hour at a time, but then 2-4 sessions per day some days. I have tried two other programs, but I have found that they present vocabulary that is far too advanced far too early.

5. Start reading (kindergarten books until mastered, then first grade books until mastered...)

To start out, find books in which the picture matches the sentence perfectly. For example, "The house is red" with a picture of a red house and almost nothing else on the page. Then, advance one step at a time with mastery. Stephen Krashen talks about mastery being the stage in which you know roughly 95% of the words on the page without difficulty. This reading needs to be a major portion of the work that is being done every day.

6. Focus on present tense

Do not worry about teaching any tense other than present tense until the student has at least 1500 words. By the way, within the 1500 words there will be some past and future tense words. This aligns well with the crawl, walk, run model. That is, instead of worrying about every possible verb in past, present and future, you can teach the student (likely within the first few hundred words) the following: before/yesterday, today/now, and tomorrow/later. This allows the student to express (even if grammatically incorrect), the past, present and future.

7. Teach the next 750 (751-1500) most frequently used words

This next set of words will be coming with the Rosetta Stone (or other system), in all likelihood. However, you need to make sure that they are there. Therefore, you need to work through the program and make cards for any of the words that are not within the program.

Also, this is a great time in which to encourage the students to learn any words that are of interest to them and that they are seeing on a regular basis (yet, the words might not be in your teaching/materials).

8. Create a "cheat" sheet

This is looking into the stumbling blocks a language learner faces at each of the levels and providing them information ahead of time. For example, at the crawl level (from Spanish to English) a student would greatly benefit from knowing as soon as possible that the la, lo, las, and los all turn into "the." At the walk level, a student learning English will greatly benefit from learning many of the past and future tenses of the most common verbs. At the run level, a student going from English to Spanish will need to know about many of the common "markers" that indicate that the subjunctive form of the verb is required.

9. Don't correct grammar or pronunciation, unless absolutely necessary (follow the crawl, walk, run model) until after they have mastered the first 1500 words

This is pretty self-explanatory and makes more sense after reading the why.

The "Whys"

1. Master the first 750 most frequently used words as fast as possible

It is virtually impossible to create meaningful sentences in any language without using some of these words. The first 100 words, as noted above, make up roughly 50% of all spoken and written language. Therefore, the faster that these words are learned, the faster all the other puzzle pieces will start to make sense. It is like building the foundation of a house before putting in the wiring. The wiring in this case could be those Common Core words that folks think are super important (and they might be). However, those apply to someone who already speaks the noted language. And, without the foundational words of the first 1500 words, there is little or nothing to help make sense of those "important" words. For example, if you want to teach the word photosynthesis (a profoundly important word that we use on a regular basis), it would be hard to do this without knowing words like: sun, energy, food, transfer, green...

2. Learn or Expose the Learner in a crawl, walk, run model

This is all about building the structure in a way that makes sense and will lead to functional language skills. A review of numerous articles and videos by language acquisition experts agreed that focusing on grammar too early slows or paralyzes the learning process. Think about your experience trying to learn a new language in either high school or college. If you had a teacher who focused on doing grammar exercises, it is highly unlikely that you actually achieved a functional level in that language. In contrast, my personal Spanish teacher focuses on present tense mastery before any significant travel into other tenses. She taught AP Spanish at a school in which her students passed the AP Spanish exam at a level 5, at a rate multiple times above the national average.

3. Teach the letter sounds, focusing on differences and tricks for mastery

This helps the student immensely with their early and later levels of reading, but also then transfers into the likelihood that their speaking will be done with more correct enunciation of the words. It is profoundly difficult to say the words correctly when you are struggling with which sounds the letters make. As I learn German, my pronunciation of words that start with v is way easier when I remember to say it like f.

4. Utilize technology as a tool every day, but not as a substitute for a teacher

There are folks that believe that Rosetta Stone is kind of boring. I have looked into this, and the number one complaint is that it is repetitive. That brings up a question: Is there anything in which you will ever be really good at without repetition? Rosetta Stone and similar programs do an amazing job of exposing the student to new words and repeating the new words in different ways, and then later circling back to the words to make sure you remember them. It is an awesome tool to help you learn the most important words (and a few extra words along the way). Repetition is a key to new learning, repetition in a way that is comprehensible is key, and comprehensible content is key. Therefore, the pictures within Rosetta Stone have created both repetition and made it comprehensible for us. Stephen Krashen is a leading expert on language acquisition, so reading his work on comprehensible input is helpful. In section two there are the names of three videos that provide wonderful information from Dr. Krashen.

5. Start reading (kindergarten books until mastered, then first grade books until mastered...)

Reading does many things for us. First, you can take a book with you virtually anywhere you go, unlike other sources of language access. Second, it is great for repetition and comprehensible input. Third, it helps the learner (if we stick with skill level appropriate books) work on building the fluency of putting the words together in sentences. Last, the research shows that our higher-level vocabulary, our higher-level grammar, and our higher-level language structures come to us through reading. The research shows that learners who read are much more likely to feel comfortable speaking and will speak more.

A grade school student usually reads about 100 words per minute and a college student reads about 300 words per minute. If your student reads 10 minutes per day, at 100 words per minute, they would read about 365,000 words per year. If they read 30 minutes per day, at 100 words per minute, they would exceed 1,000,000 words per year. Imagine the impact!

6. Focus on present tense

This is all about crawling before walking and walking before running. If you make sure that the student has the words noted above (yesterday/before, today/now, and tomorrow/later), they can express themselves without the stress of trying to learn 6, or 15, or 19 verb tenses (noting that very few native speakers use all of the tenses). The faster that a person is using a language in a manner that is successful, the more motivated they will be to learn more. And, the research has shown that the motivation* of the learner and their rate of learning are highly correlated. Within all of these steps, always look for motivational strategies. Motivation, and what improves it, varies greatly from person to person. However, higher motivational levels always lead to better learning.

*Motivation is discussed in section two, with a focus on comprehensible input and compelling content leading to motivated learners.

7. Teach the next 750 (751-1500) most frequently used words

In most languages (see the second note for the curious folks), the first 1500 most frequently used words represent 85-95% of the words used in all written and spoken language. Therefore, the faster you learn these words the more likely you are to not only understand what you hear and read, the more likely you are to have a solid enough foundation to either learn a new word or figure out a new word from context. One study indicated that knowing the first 2500 most frequently used words in any language allows one to have almost any conversation, if one is rather creative. Another study indicated that if you have a mastery of the first 4,000-5,000 most frequently used words in another language that you could attend college classes in that language. Knowing the most frequently used words is the door that opens up access to the language. When I was learning Spanish, a person who sat next to me for a couple of years in class is a polyglot. When he moved to Japan to work, they handed him a set of cards and told him, "The faster you learn these words the faster you will understand Japanese." He told me that they were all just very common words. He used that same technique moving forward.

8. Create a "cheat" sheet

This is all about saving yourself and the student a lot of frustration and heartache. There are rules in EVERY language that are weird and/or illogical. If you use the word "cuando" in Spanish (for a future action that is not a habitual action), you must make the verb subjunctive. In German, the only one of the him/her/it that changes when you have the akkusativ case is the "him." In English, "read" is both present and past tense, depending upon the context/content of the sentence, yet pronounced differently.

The cheat sheet should start out with the simplest of things. From step three in this list, letter sounds, differences and tricks is the beginning of the cheat sheet! You might want to build this with your students, working on it a little each day. Then, you can save your example for other students to use as models in the future.

9. Don't correct grammar or pronunciation, unless absolutely necessary (follow the crawl, walk, run model)

Unless it is truly critical, don't do it! If it can wait until a little later, let it wait!

It is painful and embarrassing at times to learn a new language. You will be making mistakes at an epic rate. And, if someone is correcting each and every mistake (or even a large percentage of mistakes), you sure won't make it very far into the material. Then, your confidence and desire levels will go down, and, there will be poor results for everyone involved.

Instead, encourage conversation. Help when needed. Ask questions as needed. Talk to the student about what level of correction they are comfortable with (and watch their body language to see if they were really telling the truth). The more a language is used, the easier it is to shape the language into what you are looking for (grammatically, etcetera). Therefore, too much correction is highly counterproductive to the final outcome that is desired. The final outcome should always be about functional language skills.

Who is this guy?

I was and am a teacher, just different subjects nowadays. I am a school psychologist, a trainer, a professional speaker, and someone fascinated by languages. In my early forties, I began the journey of learning Spanish, due to a huge desire to figure out why so many Spanish speaking students were over qualified for special education. I studied Spanish intensely and I am now in the DELE level C2 (check out their information, it is roughly the college level of a native speaker. Although that is a little misleading). My journey then led to graduate school again, but this second time in studying language learners. That journey led to me creating the ELL Critical Data Process. The ELL Critical Data Process is a system used to determine if the struggles a language learner is having are primarily due to normal language acquisition challenges or if they could additionally have a disability. This work led to writing eight books related to that topic with the help of my wife. Now, I am in my mid-fifties and learning German. I am trying to apply all the lessons that I have learned over these years to my new learning. Two weeks into this journey I was starting to put together simple sentences in German and was reading two simple books (late kindergarten to early first grade level).

Notes for the curious minds

Note 1: Word frequency

In order for a word frequency list to have any validity, it should have been created using computer analysis of text. However, once you get past the first 500/700 words, the text that is chosen can influence the list that you are going to see. The studies that I have read have used enough text to have 10,000,000 to 20,000,000 words to analyze. Even with that quantity of text, there were a lot of differences once the frequency lists passed about the 3,000th word. Part of the problem is the words past that point tend to be more and more topic specific. So, if there was more text related to business, then you would see more words from business. The same applies to sports, and fiction versus non-fiction can impact the lists. The good news is that you know that there will be some differences. The better news is that once you pass roughly the 1,500th word you should focus on the words that your students see more often. You and your students have likes and interests, and the more interested you are the more likely you are to see and learn the word. Remember to re-read the last few lines replacing "you" with "your student" or the reverse (which is true throughout the booklet) if you are both a language learner and/or a teacher of language learners.

Some of the studies have indicated that the words from the 5,000th to 10,000th most frequently used words are in the once every 200,000 to a million words of text range. However, that changes dramatically if it is your interest area in which the word is likely to appear. Also, the actively used vocabulary of a well-educated adult is estimated at around 10,000. This is a topic that is debated, though, due to word frequency problems, and trying to study this area in depth is very challenging. For example, imagine trying to measure the size of a person's vocabulary. Then, imagine trying to measure the size of hundreds of people's vocabularies to achieve an average, knowing that each person is likely to range from roughly 2,500 to 25,000 words.

Note 2: Percentage of language represented by most frequently used words:

This is another topic that is rather difficult to measure. I have seen studies that indicate anywhere from 85% to 95% for the first 1,500 words. But, the bottom line is that these words are critical building blocks and the foundation for building vocabulary.

Note 3: Example reference/source for most frequently used words, with the introduction on top of the page:

I simply searched for "the most frequently used words in English." With the introduction below it is easy to see why those first 100 words are so critical!

One website that comes up is shabanali.com and the information below is quoted from the first page I opened.

"Instant Words

1,000 Most Frequently Used Words

These are the most common words in English, ranked in frequency order. The first 25 make up about a third of all printed material. The first 100 make up about half of all written material, and the first 300 make up about 65 percent of all written material. Is it any wonder that all students must learn to recognize these words instantly and to spell them correctly also?

Source: The Reading Teacher's Book of Lists, Fourth Edition, © 2000 by Prentice Hall Authors: Fry, Kress & Fountoukidis"

Linking Part One to Part Two

We want to be successful in our language learning, and we want our students to be successful in their language learning. A key to success is success. It is easy to build on success and virtually impossible to build on failure. If we, or our students, are finding success in what we are doing, we are much more likely to continue. If we enjoy what we are doing, we are also much more likely to continue on that path. Language learning is a long path that requires a great deal of work. Therefore, setting ourselves, and our students, up for success with a systematic approach to building the foundation is critical. One of the huge barriers to learning a new language is frustration, or affect (part two discusses "affect" as related to language learning). So, removing as many of those barriers as is possible leads to lower frustration and higher levels of success. Then, helping each individual find their most enjoyable way/path to bridge the gap between simple conversations (the foundation) and mastery is critical. More effort will go into that final portion, the mastery, than most people imagine. Part two of this booklet is about moving from foundational learning to mastery (or whatever level you choose beyond foundational learning).

Building the foundation of language acquisition might not be as fun for some learners as other learners. Learning a new language is challenging. However, the better the methodology, the higher the likelihood of success. And, successful learners tend to have a better time learning. In the videos noted, later in part two, Dr. Krashen talks about the challenge of content being both comprehensible and compelling (enjoyable/fun). Also in part two, there is a section about the concept of "noise." That section can help many learners better understand the transitional stage most learners pass through from foundational learner toward language mastery.

The takeaway from this linking page is: foundation building is about success, success builds on success. Also, this strong foundation will increase the likelihood of comprehensible input and relevance coming sooner to the learner. The sooner the learner can access the content of their liking, the more likely they are to make the learning a daily habit, again increasing their likelihood of success.

Part Two

Moving Forward into Your Future

Introduction

Moving past the foundation of language learning is a huge journey. Many countries struggle to effectively teach additional languages. English is taught in the public schools in Spain at all levels, with very little mastery (that is not just based upon personal experience and feedback, but I have read articles in Spanish magazines talking about why they believe this is occurring). Many Asian countries teach English in their schools at all levels with very little success. But, what is success and when does it occur?

There is a saying in language learning communities: it takes 20% of the energy to get 80% of the journey toward a new language completed, and the additional 80% of the energy to get the journey 100% completed. So, again, what is success?

That is a very personal question. I have watched every video I could find from polyglots talking about language acquisition and I have read many articles and books written on this topic. Some people believe that success is being able to have a basic conversation in the target language, some people believe that success is being able to fully function in the target language. There are many studies out there that say that over 50% of the world is bilingual and about 14% of the world speaks 3 or more languages. Francois Grosjean, a linguistics expert, wrote the following in his book *Bilingual*, "So, how many bilinguals are there? Even though I have worked in the field for many years, I still haven't found a good answer. Like many others, I have reported that half of the world's population, if not more, is bilingual. But the data we all would like to have are missing." I have had the privilege of travelling to several countries and interacting with people from many more countries. My Spanish teachers alone represent 7 countries. In this, I believe that the 50% represent people who can hold a very basic conversation in another language. But, again, what do you want from your other language(s)?

As you read this, remember to replace "you" with "your student" and vice versa. Like in part one of this booklet, this is meant for the adult language learner and the teachers/program specialists/program directors of language learners.

<u>Key takeaway from this section</u>: the journey is personal, so make it personal!

Joy

There are many in the language acquisition world who will argue that it is highly unlikely that you will learn another language without enjoying the journey. However, this is again more complex than that surface level statement. There are times in which the purpose or need for the new language is greater than the joy. In the end, combining the two is best when possible.

Going backwards for a minute to make a point... Many people around the world believe that the United States is a monolingual country. However, we have over 400 languages spoken in our schools, and that likely means over 400 languages spoken in United States homes. The United States is tied for the second largest country in the world physically (with Canada and behind Russia, so you don't have to Google it). During my travels, I have heard many Europeans talk about travelling in the US some day and what they want to do (e.g., visit a friend in Texas, rent a car to visit another friend in Chicago for the weekend...) not realizing how large the United States really is. Some folks don't understand why some countries have people who speak multiple languages as a norm while others don't. For reference sake, Italy is roughly the size of the state of Arizona. Within the United States, if you live in a rural area, it is unlikely that you could have regular exposure to a language other than English as an English speaker within your community. In contrast, there are many smaller European countries in which learning a second or third language is natural and normal, given those languages are spoken all around you at all times. So, you don't have to look for the joy in language learning if you have it as a natural part of your life and potentially as a need to function in your society. Additionally, many individuals from geographically small countries need multiple languages to have successful careers.

In contrast, within a country (or a portion of a country), when there is very little access on a regular basis to your target language, you will need joy/enjoyment to make learning likely to occur.

English language learners in our schools, based on data I have collected from over 600 school districts across five states, have a far greater average level of success in learning English if their language is uncommon in the community. In all cases in which I have had the data for LTELs (long-term English Learners), the students who are not passing the state language acquisition test at the "normal" rate have all been students from the largest language groups within their setting. In most cases, within the city there are grocery stores, mechanics, doctors, etc... that function within that specific language. So, in order to have success with these student groups the school needs to not only find a way to make the language an enjoyable experience but also a meaningful experience. It is important to help individuals, students, see the doors that can open for them in their future if they have the ability to speak, and potentially function, in multiple languages.

Going back to us grown-ups who tried to learn another language in school, even college, and "failed." In most cases we failed due to ineffective methodology (grammar or skills building methodology). But, we also failed because we didn't have much use for the language in our daily lives and we didn't have a "love" for the language. I received straight A's in high school and college Spanish, but I learned nothing. I couldn't read a simple sentence and I couldn't hold a simple conversation. And, I am not alone. During the trainings I conduct, I have had about 5,000 people with similar experiences to mine try to read a simple sign in Spanish, and to date 6 people have read the sign successfully. The review I conducted of numerous articles and videos regarding language acquisition failure had the following conclusions regarding failure:

1) A lack of need for the language
2) A lack of incentive internally or externally (e.g., job, pay, cartoons, friends, etc.)
3) Methodologies that focused on grammar too early
4) Lack of practice of new skills
5) Search for the "perfect method"
6) Emotions of the learner (negative or distressing environment)
7) Focus on methodology versus acquisition that is natural

Key takeaway from this section: find the learning method that you enjoy and do it every single day.

Affective Filter

Stephan Krashen is the source if you want to know more about affective filter, and I put this note here into the paper for multiple reasons. The affective filter is related to having joy/enjoyment while learning. In a nutshell, if you put a student under the wrong types of stress during learning (i.e., have the negative impact on their affect such that they are in distress (versus stress) or making them hate the topic), then your and your students' results will be poor. As an individual learner, this goes back to making sure a big portion of your learning is enjoyable and you want to do every single day. As a teacher, this speaks to the environment you create within the classroom and the work that is done to impact the desire to learn the new language outside the classroom. Make the learning fun and make the learning meaningful in their lives, then you will see stronger learning occurring.

Please do read the work and research by Dr. Krashen on this topic. It is separated from "Joy" above because understanding nuances can help teachers, students, and adult learners. For example, understanding the difference between stress and distress as related to learning.

During the writing of this booklet I received questions regarding motivation and its role in language acquisition. The concept of motivation fills many books. My issue is that people believe that someone who is not engaged and/or not involved is not "motivated." I believe this to be far too simplistic and to potentially harmful. Instead, a person could present as "unmotivated" due to the environment they are in, their emotions, and their perception of these. So, I urge the reader to first examine potential barriers and to almost never look at a lack of learning as a lack of motivation.

Videos on YouTube featuring Dr. Krashen:

1) Stephen Krashen: What Choices Have We? Textbook vs Storybook

2) Steve Kaufman: Stephen Krashen, An Interview

3) Stephen Krashen on Language Learning in the Polyglot Community

These videos are interesting and provide an opportunity to hear the leading expert discuss the topic. Additionally, in the first video he references and provides data from research to support information in this booklet. The second video includes another expert in the field, Steve Kaufman. The third video has an interesting discussion on accents and some discussion of the polyglot "world." Throughout the booklet I have provided the following experts to investigate further: Stephen Krashen, Francois Grosjean, Noam Chomsky, Steven Kaufman, and Frederick Bodmer. I have focused the most on Dr. Krashen for three primary reasons: I am an avid reader and that is a primary focus of his work, throughout his videos he always references other experts (providing us the opportunity to dive deeper), and there are a lot of YouTube interviews of Dr. Krashen (my attention span is loving these 15-30 minute videos).

Key takeaway from this section: We aren't making it fun, just to make it fun. Reducing the negative affect as related to distress, anxiety and/or failure increases the learning.

"Noise"

If you have listened to another language that you do not know, it sounded just like noise to you. Within the language acquisition world this word is used to describe the portion of the input that you are receiving from your new language that you don't understand. What is often left out of the discussion is that some learners can proceed with a great deal of "noise" and others cannot. This could, in part, be due to the affective filter that was discussed above. In any case, as a new language learner or a teacher of new language learners, it is important to help people know that this is going to occur, it is natural, and we can adjust the content so that the quantity of "noise" you are facing is within the acceptable range for your affect. So, whether it is watching a video in the target language or reading a book in the target language, some learners can learn when 40% of the content is new to them and some learners need 10% or less of the content to be new to them (the new content is often the "noise"). As a new learner or teacher of new learners, make these adjustments to keep the affect from having a negative impact on the joy/enjoyment. Then, the likelihood of the learner wanting to engage in their learning each and every day will increase.

Key takeaway from this section: The transition from foundational learning toward language mastery brings out the challenge of finding comprehensible and compelling content. Each person has a different threshold for the "noise." So, the search for finding your personally comprehensible and compelling content is the key to a faster transition through this stage.

Daily Access

No matter the method you choose, make sure that it is both enjoyable and easy to access. A bit of work on your new language every single day is far more important than a lot of work on occasion. For me, I love to read. Therefore, I worked very hard in my new language (German) to achieve enough vocabulary as fast as possible in order to start reading. I am two months into this journey (as I wrote this sentence) and I am reading little kids books that are designed for parents to read to their children (e.g., first day of kindergarten stories) and I am reading a couple of books that are designed to focus on the most frequently used words in German. As an example, I split my practice each day into short sessions of about 15-30 minutes each: reading, Rosetta Stone, flash cards, YouTube videos. This is solely to build a foundation quickly and you could spend less time on each activity. Design the practice so that you will do it every day.

From watching and reading the experts and the polyglots, I have heard about people who love flash cards, people who love watching their favorite shows in the target language, people who learn a few words and then just go and try to converse, and more. As you have noted, I am a huge fan of using reading to increase your language skills. If you watch these folks and read their articles, you will get more and more ideas of methods to try. Keep track of what you enjoy and do it every single day.

On a side note, listen to folks who have had success learning new languages: It doesn't matter how much you read about this topic if you don't actually give it a try and have some success.

Key takeaway from this section: Find a learning method you enjoy and do it every single day!

Languages are acquired, and learned, not taught!

This is going to make some folks really upset. However, it is only because they think this means that we don't need teachers. Instead, this means that we need to do things differently. We need to make sure that our students find (or we find with them) what works on the individual level, what is enjoyable, and what will then be sustained.

What does it mean that languages are acquired, and learned, not taught? Looking at the rate of success for language acquisition when the focus is on the teaching and not the learning should be enough evidence to prove that point. But, it is a bit more complex. Think about how a baby/toddler can produce one or more languages at a level better than most college students who are studying the language. The baby/toddler cannot explain the grammar rules, but the college student can explain subjunctive to a native speaker in many cases (in English, on paper…..). Our babies and toddlers, all around the world, acquire languages with very little instruction. And, if you try to give instruction when they are not developmentally ready for it they will look at you like you are a fool. This does not mean to avoid teaching grammar. Instead, grammar should be of low importance at first, allowed to be acquired, and taught when developmentally ready.

How, then, can we not look like fools as students and teachers of new languages? We can do this by making sure that all the pieces are in place for acquisition and by focusing less on grammar. The first portion of this booklet provides information along those lines. For some people, it will be making sure they have books in which they are successful. For some people, it will be making sure they know where to find videos they will enjoy. For some people, it will be having enough card stock for the thousands of flash cards they will want to make. For other people, it might be having information on other methods to try, until they find a method that gives them daily access (with understanding/comprehension) to their target language.

<u>Key takeaway for this section</u>: Focus on finding a source that provides you or your learner a way to acquire their language!

A Little More About Acquisition

Part one of this booklet has information regarding this, with a reference to Stephen Krashen. I highly recommend reading about his work or watching the videos noted above. You will find in one of the videos he mentions numerous individuals who have completed work he finds compelling. I was very fortunate enough to have dinner with him many years ago, and he changed my language learning path in a matter of minutes.

At that time, I was studying Spanish for the third time (high school, college, and college again in my 40's). In all settings, I got A's in every single Spanish class, yet I couldn't speak, read, or function in Spanish. Two months into learning German (right now), I have more functional skills in German right now than I had in Spanish when I met Dr. Krashen (and, I had two years in high school and two years total in college). So, what is the difference? Dr. Krashen explained that I needed a source for my Spanish in which I would have comprehensible input, so that acquisition would occur. He told me to buy kindergarten books and read them until I understood them, then first grade, second grade, and so on. Understanding them meant, roughly, that I could open the book to any page and understand 95-97% of the words. I did this and within a year I had made such massive gains it was astounding to me and my teachers. And, I wasn't working any harder than before.

As a side note, there are many polyglots who will argue that you don't even need to understand the input at first, just keep going and it will occur. I will argue that knowing the first 1000 most frequently used words in the language, and reading comprehensible input, is the way to go. But, remember, you must find what works for you or your student. And, it is likely to be what you enjoy and access every single day.

<u>Key takeaway for this section</u>: Make the input comprehensible and the acquisition will occur more smoothly!

Need and Curiosity

As noted above, a need for a language can really change the learning equation. For example, I have seen many newcomer students within the school who speak a rare language acquire English very quickly. They all said the same thing to me when asked about their experience. They wanted to be able to play with the other kids and watch the cartoons (or age appropriate shows their friends talked about). Adult learners often don't have a need for the new language. So, what if you don't have a need, but just a want? For me, I want to learn another language for three main reasons: 1) I really need something to keep my brain busy and me out of trouble, 2) Learning new languages has been shown to keep older brains healthier and to slow issues like Alzheimer's, 3) I really wanted to test out the information I had gathered over the years regarding language acquisition. The onset of the COVID 19 pandemic left me with extra time, so I decided to move forward with learning a new language. Each adult learner needs to find their reason for the new language that gives them enough energy to make sure they will practice their new language every single day. For some people, that can just be the curiosity about the culture that surrounds that language. For other people, it might be the curiosity about English and how it came about. Learning either a romance language or a Germanic language provides a lot of insight into English. As I learn German I am shocked when I come across a new word (a word that I don't know) and then, when pronounced correctly, the meaning is obvious. For example, pronounce the following word with an "f" for the "v" and a long "a" for the second "e:" vergeben.

<u>Key takeaway for this section</u>: if you don't have a need, find a curiosity!

YouTube Videos

The availability of language videos on YouTube regarding learning the language you want to learn, examples of the language you want to learn, TV shows in the language you want to learn, Ted Talks on language acquisition, and talks in general from polyglots is simply amazing. Like anything on the internet, use a little caution regarding the information. I always look to triangulate, meaning that I don't tend to believe the information until I have found 3 or more independent sources providing the same information. Even then, you still need to see if it makes sense and works for you. This information though, has helped me with my German at an incredible level. Each week I run into something that just drives me a little crazy. Luckily, I am not the first person doing this and there is almost always a video that explains the problem, why it is a problem for an English speaker going to German, and the solution. Additionally, I find the polyglots fascinating to listen to. However, take a little bit of caution with polyglots. I have found that some really don't understand how normal folks learn, but some do a great job of providing information across a variety of potential learners.

I see YouTube as offering great content for language learners in at least the following four areas:

1) Level appropriate videos for listening
2) Language learning strategies, including and beyond those I have mentioned
3) Problem solving (if something is confusing, there is often a video to help with understanding)
4) Grammar --- Although I am not a big fan, there are a lot of 5-15 minute videos that make learning about grammar more bite sized

The services like Netflix, Prime Video, and Disney also have a great deal of content in many languages. The children's shows are written at an easier level, the speakers usually speak slightly slower, and the speakers usually take a great deal of effort to pronounce the words correctly.

Key takeaway for this section: YouTube is your friend, if you are careful and thoughtful about using it.

Aging

As mentioned above, learning a new language or learning how to play the piano have been shown to be highly effective methods to slow the aging process of the brain. As we grow older, our brains struggle with flexible thinking. The process of switching between languages requires exercise in flexible thinking, potentially slowing the deterioration in this area. Do some research on this topic and see the studies.

Key takeaway for this section: I am getting old…. Or, language learning is exercise for your brain!

Switching Gears

The following portion of this booklet focuses on individual topics. Each of the topics is related to the process of being a language learner, either individually or as a teacher helping a language learner to be successful.

What is your goal for learning a new language?

This is something that you should work toward discovering early on in the process of learning a language. There are some people who would love to know a little bit of a language, or several languages, so that they can say a few phrases or hold a very simple conversation when in another country. There are people who want to be able to function within the new language at a professional level. Then, there is everyone in-between.

Why is this important? The main reason for this is with regards to how much effort one puts into grammar. I will argue that no matter what your answer is, you should not prioritize grammar until later stages of learning. I have seen many language learners become completely paralyzed while trying to figure out a grammar or tense issue. Instead, as noted much earlier, learn some ways to get around this at first and let it absorb.

If you just want to hold the simplest of conversations, you can function completely in present tense and just use the words earlier/yesterday, now/today, later/tomorrow. In contrast, functioning at a professional level will require the ability to create complex structures, like correct usage of subjunctive. Knowing this within the process helps you to know whether or not to put effort into grammar, or to just allow the necessary grammar to absorb through acquisition.

Key takeaway for this section: Make goals and work toward them, yet be flexible along the way.

Goals for Your Students

Luckily, you should be able to access language standards from your state department that will help to guide this discussion. However, what if you get a newcomer who is 17 and needs to work to help the family pay the bills? If you could help this young person understand the doors that open via learning English, you might completely change the course of their life. And, doing this isn't about telling them they have to learn English. Instead, it is all about helping them see opportunity and helping them see an enjoyable path to learning English. Some of these students clearly know this, yet are under pressure to help support their families. What can you do to support them, even if they leave school? I would suggest creating a short document in their language with many of these ideas and the related resources.

How does this relate to the little ones? There is a famous graph that shows we learn listening, speaking, reading and writing in that order. It makes sense, but is it true? The graph shows up under images by googling "language acquisition listening speaking reading writing." An odd thing occurs when searching for this graph. The ELL Critical Data Process, my process, is linked to this graph, even though I never used this graph in my presentations. There is research by Dr. Krashen that shows that working on reading leads to increased speaking. That was my personal experience.

The point of this discussion is that the learning needs to be personalized to the student. Some students will show their gifts in different ways. Therefore, don't allow "inside the box thinking" to keep a student from making progress.

During the writing of this booklet, the question arose regarding learning a language being such a social process. In other words, if you want to speak a language well you will likely need to socialize with native speakers of the language. Again, this is a highly individualized topic. Some learners and students will never struggle to socialize, some will need encouragement. For individuals who are not as socially motivated, there are lots of ways to begin this process via the internet (e.g., using Zoom or the equivalent to trade language time with someone who wants to learn English but lives in a remote area of their country and doesn't have access to English speakers).

Key takeaway for this section: Help your students to find good goals for them, that are meaningful and enjoyable.

Words Needed in the Target Language

This has been discussed regarding building a foundation or basic conversation. However, if your goal is that of a native speaker level you will need much higher levels of vocabulary. Additionally, two big challenges arise when you try to research this topic. First, how are we counting the words? For example, are tough, tougher, toughest, toughness four words? Or, one word? In German when the past tense has virtually no resemblance to the present tense of a word, is that two words? In German, when they make a verb into a noun by changing the ending, is that one word? Then, the second challenge is measuring vocabulary. There is NO effective way to measure the active and passive vocabulary of a well-educated adult. There are programs and sites that claim to do this, but it is just an estimate. So, the estimate is that you need at least 2,500 words in a target language to have a variety of conversations. Then, the DELE system level C2 is estimated to be a vocabulary of at least 16,000 words in the target language (the C2 level is the highest of their levels and roughly represents the language skills of a well-educated adult in a given language). If you have done any research on word frequency you will know that the words past the 5,000th word in frequency are actually very rare in conversation or text, unless they are from your area of study and you are reading/speaking within that area.

Key takeaway for this section: You will be able to function on a simple level with just a couple thousand of words in your target language, but you will need a great deal more work on vocabulary to reach a "mastery" level.

Secondary Students and Heritage Language Programs

It has been a huge surprise to me how many people involved in the EL world have never heard about heritage language programs (and outside the EL world, nobody has heard about these). This is simply teaching a subject (history, math, etc.) in the native language of your students. Obviously, this requires enough students who speak a language to make it work. However, it is so well developed for Spanish that there are already textbooks available to buy.

Culture is closely tied to language and the addition of a heritage language program helps our students see that their language is valued, which leads to placing a value on their culture.

If you are teaching a heritage language class, one suggestion I would make is to create one assignment per week in which the students complete the assignment in English. Then, have a class discussion regarding the tricks, skills, and transferable skills (from their native language) that the students used in order to accomplish completing the assignment in English. In other words, help them to discover their transferable skills.

Note: Heritage language programs vary in definition, with some being all about achieving literacy in the heritage/native language.

Key takeaway for this section: We have an amazing opportunity with Heritage Language classes!

Immersion

Some people talk about language immersion and do not realize what is really occurring. What they are imagining is a structured learning environment in which all or almost all of the content is in the target language, which is often not the case. There is a great deal of information available on immersion and language learners, and this booklet is not focused on that topic. Instead, the purpose of mentioning immersion here is to make sure that the reader understands that they or their student need direct instruction that is targeted at acquiring the new language, growing the skills of listening, speaking, reading and writing in the new language, instead of throwing them into a pool even though they can't swim, and hope for the best.

Takeaway: see below

SIOP and GLAD

These are methods taught to teachers and used by teachers in order to increase the likelihood that a student will comprehend a lesson. I fully support the usage of these skills and techniques. I have included these here, though, to make sure we don't forget that this is not actually teaching English, but making English more accessible. The reason for this will become apparent a couple of paragraphs later.

Takeaway: see below

Academic Conversations

Academic conversations is a hot area within the language learner world and a very valuable tool. This is included, like the paragraph above, to help the reader understand that this is a tool and not specifically teaching English.

Takeaway: see below

What I have seen, both in the EL and Special Education Worlds

I have been fortunate to have worked with educators from many states, maybe all the states. In both special education and English Learning, direct instruction has fallen behind greatly. I can say that the most common thing I see occurring in the EL world is helping students finish assignments and that the same is extremely common within the special education world for secondary students who are not significantly impaired by their disability.

Within both of these worlds, the usage of the money that is received to provide services is clearly delineated in some format or law. For example, if a student who receives special education has an area of specially designed instruction listed for reading, then they must receive a service in reading that is outlined within their IEP. Therefore, helping them finish homework from a variety of classes will never meet that goal. Nor will some accommodations or modifications.

Within the English Learner world, the money that is received to provide a service is for increasing listening, speaking, reading and writing until the student can pass the state examination in those areas. So, a general education teacher using SIOP and/or GLAD strategies is likely to help the student acquire skills in some of the areas, but unlikely to help the student meet the bar noted above (i.e., specifically growing their skills in listening, speaking, reading and writing so that they can meet the state requirements).

Having academic conversation is an interesting topic. If the student is interested and/or motivated, this is likely to be indirectly and sometimes directly related to increases in all the noted areas. Also, using the new language skills in a functional manner is extremely important to overall language growth. However, it isn't a targeted strategy for either reading or writing. None of this would be a problem if English Learning was well funded; however, it isn't. Therefore, decisions must be made and these decisions often leave some portion of the educational puzzle without a direct service. I will argue that direct service, to achieve the goals noted in the first portion of this booklet on building the foundation, are where the bulk of the available money should be spent. Then, help educators as a whole understand the need for the information from the second portion of the booklet with remaining funds. In other words, help the student build their foundation (with direct instruction) and help them find their most effective pathway toward learning (indirect instruction or general education support). To initially build a skill (the foundation) the learner needs to know what they are learning, they need direct instruction on the skill, and there needs to be a "check" for learning to know whether or not re-learning is needed. This varies by individual, regarding the time and quantity, but discovery method or immersion is NOT effective for language acquisition.

<u>Key takeaways for the sections immediately above</u>: It would be incredible if we could do everything we know to help our language learners to advance. However, we have some limitations that have been put upon us. Therefore, thoughtful decisions need to be made and evidence (data) must be used to make sure our decisions are actually leading to the best outcomes for our students. Saying that something you are doing is research driven is virtually meaningless (we could talk about this at another time). Show the evidence that your approach is working for your students in your setting, that is meaningful. Please note that I fully support SIOP, GLAD, and Academic Conversations and my concern is not about their value as tools. My concern is that we need to guarantee our language learners direct instruction that is specifically aligned to the goals of growing their skills in the four core areas. Last, direct instruction does

not equal "pull out" services, which have been shown to be ineffective. Like all things in life, there is a balance to be achieved. Part of the direct instruction can focus on the presentation and access to reading materials and listening materials that are both comprehensive and compelling. The research supports growth in all noted areas when the students have access to and support with compelling and comprehensible content.

Making Mistakes and Language Learning

It is a mistake to believe something works because somebody told you it would. And, mistakes are truly critical to the learning process. Many adult language learners have their progress paralyzed by the fear of making mistakes. Our students have less fear, but they still have some fear of making mistakes. We must encourage making mistakes as part of the learning process. However, we should be using systems that we actually know work, based upon our data. We can start out with something that is claimed to be research based, and we probably will. The reason we need our data to prove it is the following. First, the research is usually artificial to some level. For example, Co-Teaching is incredibly popular across the country, even though the leading researcher in the world on education, John Hattie, has shown it to not be highly effective. The problem isn't that Co-Teaching isn't effective in some cases (there are some studies to show it as highly effective). The problem is that it doesn't generalize across settings the way one would hope. Many research studies that support this, in all likelihood, did an amazing job of picking the correct teachers to pair together and then making sure they had the support and time to do Co-Teaching as designed. In contrast, that just isn't what happens on a regular basis in the real world.

So, we as educators must make sure that what we are doing is actually working for our students. They need to be open and willing to make mistakes, we need to be open and willing to know if and when we are making mistakes. As noted above, there isn't one way to learn a language. Yet, we need to make sure learning is actually occurring.

Key takeaway for this section: We need to be open to making mistakes and we need to encourage our students to make mistakes, yet we also need to monitor our data to know when a change is needed (meaning, learning is not occurring as hoped with the current model).

What is Bilingual or Multi-lingual?

This actually relates to making mistakes in some ways. Do you have to be "native" in two languages to be bilingual? Does the ability to have really simple conversations in three languages make you trilingual? In other words, can you still be making mistakes on a somewhat regular basis and be bilingual?

The book *Bilingual* by Francois Grosjean is a great book on this topic. Not only does he help the language learner get their head around this concept, he helps teachers understand the concerns that go along with language loss. Early in this book he notes, that when he was beginning his book, he searched the internet for the word bilingual and there were 32,000,000 results. I searched it right after writing that sentence, and I got 126,000,000 results. Pretty good likelihood that there are varied opinions within that group.

I will argue that a person needs to be able to function across a variety of settings, even with mistakes and missteps, in the new language to be able to call it "their" language. I will argue that reading and/or writing in a target language is not necessary to achieve this "title," but that a person who doesn't read in a target language will have a limited vocabulary. There is a huge difference between sounding great because you have the perfect accent and the ability to function across a variety of topics. In the end, is it important? That depends upon your goal. I have met people who only speak in the present tense in their additional languages and get all of their wants and needs met. Just a thought!

Key takeaway for this section: Nobody really agrees on the definition/characteristics required to be bilingual or multilingual, and if you are getting what you want from your new language you shouldn't care too much about the "definitions" posed by experts.

If you want to dive into language and language learning….

This is for the geeks in the group. I am reading a book that came highly recommended to me, because I kind of geek out on this topic. The book is *The Loom of Language* by Frederick Bodmer. It is not just interesting to read, but it points out some of the completely nonsensical things that exist in languages. For example, the following exists in English: I need, you need, we need, they need, she _____, he _____. There is no logical reason for this. Then, in French, there are times in which the endings of words change, in a set pattern, yet the pronunciation does not change, like many words in which an "s" is added to the word and the pronunciation remains the same. This is an older book, so it was written with some language and ideas from the 1940s (please take this warning seriously).

Additionally, reading the works of Noam Chomsky can provide interesting perspectives.

Takeaway for this section: language learning is fascinating and/or Steve is a geek

List of Takeaways

The journey is personal, so make it personal!

Find the learning method that you enjoy and do it every single day.

We aren't making it fun, just to make it fun. Reducing the negative affect increases the learning.

Each person has a different threshold for the "noise." So, the search for finding your personally comprehensible and compelling content is the key to a faster transition through this stage.

Focus on finding a source that provides you or your learner a way to acquire their language!

Make the input comprehensible and the acquisition will occur more smoothly!

If you don't have a need, find a curiosity!

YouTube is your friend, if you are careful and thoughtful about using it.

Language learning is exercise for your brain!

Make goals and work toward them, yet be flexible along the way.

Help your students to find good goals for them that are meaningful and enjoyable.

You will be able to function on a simple level with just a couple thousand of words in your target language, but you will need a great deal more work on vocabulary to reach a "mastery" level.

We have an amazing opportunity with heritage language classes!

It would be incredible if we could do everything we know to help our language learners to advance. However, we have some limitations that have been put upon us. Therefore, thoughtful decisions need to be made and evidence (data) must be used to make sure our decisions are actually leading to the best outcomes for our students. Saying that something you are doing is research driven is virtually meaningless (we could talk about this at another time). Show the evidence that your approach is working for your students in your setting, that is meaningful. Please note that I fully support SIOP, GLAD, and Academic Conversations and my concern is not about their value as tools. My concern is that we need to guarantee our language learners direct instruction that is specifically aligned to the goals of growing their skills in the four core areas. Last, direct instruction does not equal "pull out" services, which have been shown to be ineffective. Like all things in life, there is a balance to be achieved. Part of the direct instruction can focus on the presentation and access to reading materials and listening materials that are both comprehensive and compelling. The research supports growth in all noted areas when the students have access to and support with compelling and comprehensible content.

We need to be open to making mistakes and we need to encourage our students to make mistakes, yet we also need to monitor our data to know when a change is needed (meaning, learning is not occurring as hoped with the current model).

Nobody really agrees (on the definition of bilingual), and if you are getting what you want from your new language you shouldn't care too much about the "definitions" posed by experts.

Language learning is fascinating!

In a nutshell, make it fun, make it comprehensible, make sure there is easy access, and do it every single day!

Conclusions

Language learning is very challenging, unless the circumstances exist in which the language is acquired as naturally as possible. Even with the best of circumstances, most of us will need patience and kindness. The stories out there about learning a new language in a month are either silliness or those incredibly rare individuals who have a gift. Most, almost all, people will need consistent work toward learning a new language over a long period of time. You can set yourself up for success or set your students up for success by building a strong foundation and then setting your own personal path, your students' path, toward higher levels of language functioning that is a path you and/or your students not only enjoy, but is a path that you will access every single day.

Please note, there are some amazing and crucial topics within this booklet that don't get the coverage they deserve. The goal of this booklet was concrete and implementable information that is delivered in as brief of a format as possible. This is the beginning.

About the Authors

Steve Gill

Steve's first job in education, before he became a school psychologist, was as a driver's education teacher. Then Steve had a wonderful opportunity to study school psychology and work at the university, so he followed that path.

Steve started his career as a school psychologist in a district with a large ELL population. There he realized how little he had learned about language learners prior to this experience. Over the years, he completed graduate work in ELL studies, eventually creating the ELL Critical Data Process. As of writing this, Steve has trained over 12,000 educators on the process across more than 600 school districts in multiple states.

Steve is a Past President of the Washington State Association of School Psychologists.

Go to SteveGillELL.com for information on trainings.

Ushani Nanayakkara

Ushani is a writer, artist and trainer who has worked for major corporations as a training manager. Ushani has been instrumental in the writing of our books, working diligently to ensure that the writing speaks to a wider audience.

Ushani grew up speaking three languages simultaneously, as a child in Sri Lanka and then as an adolescent in German. She later learned a fourth language, which she is working to regain these days.

Publications

Steve and Ushani have six books for sale on Amazon.com. The first book, *The ELL Critical Data Process – 2nd Edition,* is a resource for learning professionals for determining whether more interventions are needed or if a special education referral is a reasonable option. Their second book, *Evaluating ELL Students for the Possibility of Special Education Qualification* went into print in September of 2015, and focuses on the special education evaluation process for language learners and how to potentially achieve appropriate identification rates. Their third book, *Special Education Referral or Not*, is about using a matrix-based approach with non-language learners. Their fourth book, *ELL Teachers and Special Education*, is a self-study or group study course for ELL teachers to learn more about special education. Their fifth book, *Processing Perspectives: Examining Beliefs, Biases, and Reality Through Stories* is a collection of educator stories and reflections that helps the reader see another way to look at an issue. Their sixth book, *Lessons Learned While Evaluating ELL Students for Potential Special Education Qualification* focuses on the educator and student during the process of the evaluation.

Acknowledgments

We would like to thank the following educators for their ideas and suggestions during our editing process: Kim Halley, Summer Holmes, Annalisa Miner, Nancy Miramontes, Mark Orr, Danielle Rhea, M. Alicia Robertson, Terryl Swejk, and Jeanne-Marie Wright.

Made in the USA
Columbia, SC
04 September 2020